I0160061

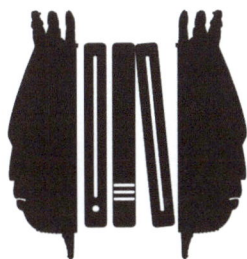

BLACK LEGACY PRESS™

WWW.BLACKLEGACYPRESS.ORG

ANANSI HOW STORIES CAME TO EARTH

AS RETOLD BY
UWA AFU

ANANSI HOW STORIES CAME TO EARTH

As Retold By
Uwa Afu

Copyright © 2023 by BLP PUBLISHING

All rights reserved. No part of this publication may be reproduced or transmitted in any form or by any means electronic or mechanical, including information storage and retrieval systems without permission in writing from the publisher, except for student research using the appropriate citations.

BLP PUBLISHING
Eastchester New York

For wholesale please visit:
www.BBWLogistics.com

Available wherever books are sold.

ISBN: 978-1-63652-124-4

Long long ago in Africa, a spider named Anansi emerged. He went everywhere, throughout the world, travelling on his strong web strings - sometimes looking more like a wise old man than a spider. Long -long time ago, there were no stories on Earth for anyone to tell. The sky-god kept all stories to himself, up high in the sky locked away in a wooden box.

These the spider wanted, as many creatures had before him, so that he could know the beginnings and endings of things. Yet all who had tried for the stories had returned empty-handed.

Anansi climbed up his web to the sky-god, Nyame, to ask for the sky-god's stories.

When the powerful sky-god saw the thin, spidery, old man crawling up to his throne, he laughed at him, "What makes you think that you, of all creatures, can pay the price I ask for my stories?"

Anansi wanted to know, "What is the price of the stories?"

"My stories have a great price, four fearsome, elusive creatures: Onini, the python that swallows men whole; Osebo, the leopard with teeth like spears; Mmoboro, the hornets that swarm and sting; and Mmoatia, the fairy who is never seen. Bring these creatures to me."

Bowing, the spider quietly turned and crept back down through the clouds. He planned to capture the four creatures he needed as price for the stories.

He first asked his wife, Aso, how he might capture Onini, the python that swallows men whole. She told him a plan, saying, "Go and cut off a branch of the palm tree and cut some string-creeper as well. Take these to the stream where python lives."

As Anansi went to the swampy stream, carrying these things, he began arguing aloud, "This is longer than he; You lie, no; it Is true; this branch is longer and he is shorter, much shorter."

The python was listening, and asked what spider was talking about, "What are you muttering, Anansi?"

14

"I tell you that my wife, Aso, is a liar, for she says that you are longer than this palm branch and I say that you are not."
Onini, the python, said, "Come and place the branch next to me and we will see if she is a liar.

And so, Anansi put the palm branch next to the python's body, and saw the large snake stretch himself alongside it. Anansi then bound the python to the branch with the string-creeper and wound it over and over - nwenene! nwenene! nwenene! - until he came to the head. Then the spiderman said to Onini, "Fool, I will now take you to the sky-god."

" This Anansi did as he spun a web around the snake to carry him back through the clouds to the sky kingdom. On seeing the gigantic snake, Nyame merely said, "There remains what still remains."

Spider came back to Earth to find the next creature, Osebo the leopard, with teeth like spears. His wife, Aso, told him, "Go dig a large hole."
Anansi said, "I understand, say no more." After following the tracks of the leopard, spider dug a very deep pit. He covered it over with the branches of the trees and came home.

"Returning in the very early morning, he found a large leopard lying in the pit. "Leopard, is this how you act? You should not be prowling around at night; look at where you are! Now put your paw here, and here, and I will help you out."

24

The leopard put his paws up on the sticks that Anansi placed over the pit and began to climb up. Quickly, Anansi hit him over the head with a wooden knife - gao! Leopard fell back into the pit - fom! Anansi quickly spun the leopard to the sticks with his web string.

"Fool, I am taking you to pay for the sky-god's stories."

But the sky-god received the leopard saying, "What remains, still remains."

Next the spiderman went looking for Mmoboro, the hornets
that swarm and sting. Spider
told his wife, Aso, what he was
looking for and she said, "Look
for an empty gourd and fill it
with water."
This spider did and he went
walking through the bush until
he saw a swarm of hornets
hanging there in a tree. He
poured out some of the water
and sprinkled it all over their
nest. Cutting a leaf from a
nearby banana tree, he held it
up and covered his head.

He then poured the rest of the water from the gourd all over himself. Then while he was dripping he called out to the hornets, "The rain has come, do you see me standing here with a leaf to cover my head? Fly inside my empty gourd so that the rain will not beat at your wings." The hornets flew into the gourd, saying, "Thank you - hhhuuummm - Aku; thank you - hhhuuummm - Ananse." Anansi stopped up the mouth of the gourd, and spinning a thick web around it, said, "Fools, I'm taking you to the sky-god as price for his stories."

Anansi knew very well what re-mained - it was the fairy, Mmoatia, who is never seen. When the spider came back to Earth, he asked Aso what to do. And so, he carved an Akua's child, a wooden doll with a black, flat face, and covered it with sticky fluid from a tree. Walking through the bush, he found the odum tree, where the fairies like to play.

He then made eto, pounded yams, and put some in the doll's hand and even more of the yams into a brass basin at her feet - there by the odum tree. Anansi next hid in the bushes, with a vine creeper in his hands that was also tied to the doll's neck.

He then made eto, pounded yams, and put some in the doll's hand and even more of the yams into a brass basin at her feet - there by the odum tree. Anansi next hid in the bushes, with a vine creeper in his hands that was also tied to the doll's neck.

It wasn't long before the fairies came, two sisters, to play. They saw the doll with the eto and asked if they could have some. Anansi made the doll's head nod, "Yes", by pulling on the string-creeper. Soon the faries had eaten all the eto and so, thanked the doll, but the doll did not reply. The fairies became angry.One sister said, "When I thank her, she says nothing." The other sister replied, "Then slap her in her crying place." This the fairy did, she slapped it's cheek - "pa!" - but her hand stuck there. She slapped it with her other hand - "pa!" - and that hand stuck, too. She kicked it with both one foot, then the other, and both feet stuck to the sticky wooden doll. Finally, she pushed her stomache to it and that stuck.

Then Anansi came from his hiding place, and said, "Fool, I have got you, and now I will take you to the sky-god to buy his stories once and for all." Anansi spun a web around the last of the four creatures and brought Mmoatia up to Nyame in the sky kingdom. The sky-god, seeing this last catch, called together all his nobles. He put it before them and told them that the spider-man had done what no-one else had been able to do.

He said in a loud voice that rang in the sky,"From now and forever, my sky-god stories belong to you - kose! kose! kose! - my blessing, my blessing, my blessing. We will now call these "Spider Stories"." And so, child, stories came to Earth because of the great cunning of Kwaku Anansi, and his wife, Aso. When Anansi brought the wooden box of stories to his home, he and his wife eagerly learned each one of them. And you can still see today that Aku and Aso tell their stories. Everywhere you look, they spin their webs for all to see.

www.ingramcontent.com/pod-product-compliance
Lightning Source LLC
Chambersburg PA
CBHW061057090426

42742CB00002B/79